We build our reputation

WHISPERS OF CHANGE

ENJOY A REWARDING NEW CAREER WITH EUROPE'S TOP TRAINING PROVIDER

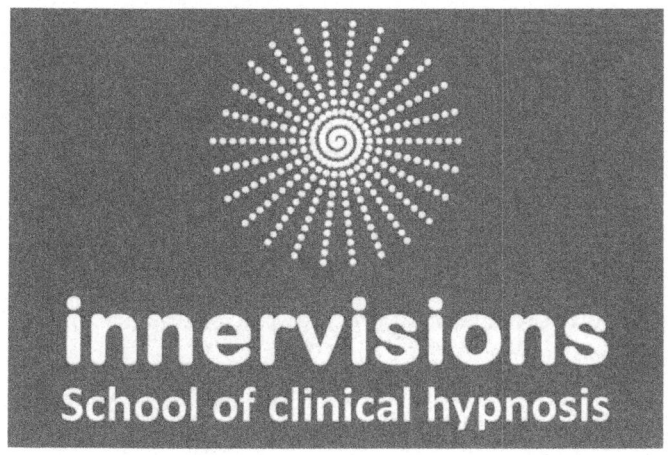

We build our reputation on your success

CONTENTS

INTRODUCTION:	3
HYPNOSIS	8
OUR UNIQUE APPROACH TO TEACHING	27
OUR VIRTUAL CLASSROOM	29
HYPNOTHERAPY AS A CAREER	31
WHAT THE PEOPLE SAY:	42
KAREN TAYLOR: HYPNOTHERAPY ECKINGTON	43
LAURA CALLAGHAN: HYPNOTHERAPY BY LAURA CALLAGHAN	45
JAYNE PADLEY: J E CLINICAL HYPNOTHERAPY	48
NICKI CLARKE: NICKI CLARK HYPNOTHERAPY	50
KAREN GOODWIN: BEAUTIFUL MINDS	53
CHERYL LAWTON: MY POSITIVE HEALTH	56
MARY BLAKEY: MARY T BLAKEY THERAPY UK	59
JACQUELINE ANDERSON: ESSENCE HYPNOTHERAPY	61
PAUL TORRINGTON: EDWARD PAUL HYPNOTHERAPY	64
HELEN JANE: HELEN JANE HYPNOTHERAPY	67
DONNA GALLOWAY: SEVEN HILLS WELLBEING CENTRE	70
VIVIENNE RAWNSLEY:	72
MICHELE KNOTT SIMEY:	75
SUE FERGUSON: SUE FERGUSON HYPNOTHERAPY	77
CAROLLE WESTBURY: INSIDE MIND HYPNOTHERAPY	80
LEAH GOODALL: LEAH GOODALL HYPNOTHERAPY	82
KELLY KING: BE FREE CLINICAL HYPNOTHERAPY	84
LEANNE DEWEY: MADE MINDSET	86
POTENTIAL EARNINGS	88
EQUAL OPPORTUNITIES	93
WHAT NEXT?	94

We build our reputation on your success

INTRODUCTION:

My name is Brian Glenn. In February 2024 I celebrated twenty-eight years as a principal of Innervisions School of Clinical Hypnosis. I conducted my very first training course in the East Yorkshire town of Goole back in 1996

It actually all started about thirty years ago, when I changed direction and became a clinical hypnotherapist, sparked by an amazing insight inspired by my father whilst performing my comedy hypnosis stage show on Blackpool Pier.

I had recently been disabled by an industrial injury where my dominant right arm was paralysed and withering away. My positive nature found a way to come to terms with my doctor's advice to amputate my arm, I was then actually looking forward to this in anticipation of being recognised as 'the one-armed hypnotist' – I even had posters printed!

My father commented on the power of the mind after attending my stage show and inspired me to use the power of my mind to repair my paralysed right arm. An amazing light bulb moment.

I studied the works of Milton Erickson MD who on two separate occasions used the power of his mind to learn to walk again following paralysis caused by polio.

The following twelve months was a turning point in my life as I used my skills to bring my arm back to around 95% recovery. I considered the industrial accident to be Karmic debt due to my rather aggressive and colourful teenage years, and spent time looking for a way to neutralise that debt. Then, a few weeks later, I woke in the earlier hours of the morning with an amazing inspirational and overwhelming message. It was in that moment that I made an agreement with myself which would eventually serve as my life's purpose whilst at the same time neutralise the Karmic debt I had accumulated as a teenager.

This was my revelation.

MY LIFE'S PURPOSE:
'TO HELP ONE MILLION DURING MY LIFETIME'

And so it began, my life became meaningful; for the first time in my life, I had a sense of purpose. I abandoned stage hypnosis, attended a basic hypnotherapy training course and opened my first hypnotherapy clinic. I also enrolled on an 'A' level Psychology course at my local college which eventually lead me to a degree in clinical psychology.

Miracles started to happen right before my eyes. I was seeing clients on a daily basis after opening a complimentary Health Centre on Hessle Road, Hull.

Still not feeling like I was doing enough to achieve my 'Million', I decided to teach other people to do the work that I did, creating a pyramid effect. This led to the birth of my training company: Innervisions School of Clinical Hypnosis.

We build our reputation on your success

Now semi-retired from hypnotherapy, and managing the business from our beautiful home in the Costa Blanca region of Spain, I am privileged and honoured to have a fantastic team of dedicated world class tutors.

Behind the scenes, I have my wonderful, loving partner, Shirley, keeping me motivated and in good spirits doing all the business related stuff that I don't like doing!

Welcome to the fascinating and wonderful world of clinical hypnosis. I hope you enjoy the contents of this book!

Take care and stay safe. And perhaps one day soon you too could become part of my million!

With love...

Brian Glenn
PRINCIPAL
INNERVISIONS SCHOOL OF CLINICAL HYPNOSIS
www.innervisions.co.uk

PREFACE

Over the past twenty-nine years, our hypnotherapy training course has evolved into one of Europe's most comprehensive resources for individuals looking to train in Modern Clinical Hypnosis.

We have a proven formula that will take you through a dedicated learning process using modern accelerated learning techniques, hosted by our world class tutors.

MODULAR TRAINING SYSTEM

The training consists of approximately 120 classroom training hours as specified by our accrediting body; The General Hypnotherapy Standards Council. In order to gain our diploma in clinical hypnosis and recommendation for full membership of GHSC, all course delegates must meet this requirement with no exceptions.

Students who are unable to attend any of the module dates will be given the opportunity to catch up on a one-to-one session with one of our tutors via Zoom.

This will be a short version of the full weekend and an additional fee will be required due to the extra tutor time commitment.

COURSE EVOLUTION

We are proud to be one of Europe's longest established training providers. Currently in our 28th year and still going strong.

This does not mean that we are still teaching the same course as we did all those years ago, indeed we update our course material and course content on every course intake.

Our tutors are constantly updating their knowledge and keeping up with major developments in the industry thus ensuring that the content always remains relevant, current and valid.

HYPNOSIS

Many of us are familiar with this scene: A bizarre-looking man holds a clock pendant and continuously, determinedly swings it in front of a vulnerable, lost-looking young woman. He utters the phrase repeatedly, in slower and lower intonation: *"You're getting sleepy... You're getting sleepy..."* The girl stares blankly into the clock. The world turns and swirls around her, spiralling and spiralling. Then eventually, she starts to act like (a) a zombie, (b) a vamp, (c) a chicken, or (d) all of the above simultaneously.

Thanks to popular culture, hypnosis has achieved an eerie, mystical, otherworldly, and sometimes evil reputation. While the scenario illustrated above may have a little ring of truth to it (hypnosis using verbal suggestion is powerful; and people under hypnosis can be made to believe and therefore act as a different identity), there is certainly a lot more about hypnosis than meets the eye.

Doubtless one of the most intriguing yet also one of the most bewildering topics to come across man, hypnosis transcends boundaries as it continues to be studied, analysed, and interpreted in diverse fields of wisdom. From medicine, psychology, new age, self-help, religion, history, media and popular culture, hypnosis is accorded with different meanings, interpretations, and uses: the conclusions never final, the reports ever-evolving.

This may be rooted from one thesis: that studying hypnosis would inevitably mean studying the human mind, and definitely the human mind is an ever-changing overlapping universe of significance, interpretation, and purpose.

In this book, we will attempt to touch on the different aspects of understanding hypnosis, and how it was and still is being utilised (or condemned by some parties), for various reasons. So, read on and judge for yourself. Join me as we try to discuss some of the major points of view regarding mind control. Explore or reject the possibility of controlling the human mind and the life of the person possessing it. But please should you decide to move further into the topic let me be clear. Nobody is controlling your decision, and anything you will be engaging in shall be done on your own free will!

WHAT HYPNOSIS CAN AND CAN'T DO

The Webster's New International Dictionary defines hypnosis as "the induction of a state resembling sleep or somnambulism, which is called hypnosis or hypnotic sleep; also loosely, the induced state of hypnosis."

There are degrees of hypnosis which have been characterised as "lethargic, cataleptic and somnambulistic hypnosis; and again, simply as light and heavy hypnotic sleep, with corresponding variations in suggestibility."

However, Encyclopaedia Britannica further states "there remains no generally acceptable explanation for hypnosis, though one prominent theory focuses on the possibility of discrete dissociative states affecting portions of consciousness."

The word hypnosis is derived from the Greek word *Hypnos*, meaning sleep. Hypnosis is often presumed to make someone go under a state of reduced consciousness while the person remains awake. The general behaviour of those under hypnosis is that subjects are extremely susceptible to suggestions and achieving a high level of relaxation.

Daydreaming is another activity likened to hypnosis wherein a person looks oblivious to his surroundings yet experiences heightened imagination (depending on how deep the trance is).

There are two ways by which hypnosis is performed: (1) hetero-hypnosis, wherein a hypnotist induces a state of being in trance and open to suggestions; and (2) auto-hypnosis, wherein the state is self-induced. The latter is also known as self-hypnosis. In actuality, all hypnosis is self-hypnosis because no hypnotist can induce hypnosis without the subject's consent. The results are the same whether induced by a hypnotist or by oneself, but some find it easier to go into hypnosis when aided by a hypnotist.

A suggestion that is carried out a period of time after hypnosis is known as a post-hypnotic suggestion.

Believe it or not, we experience hypnosis every day. Have you ever been so engrossed with a movie or a book that you did not immediately notice someone calling you at the top of his voice? Did you ever miss an exit while driving down the motorway because you were deep in thought? Were you ever caught daydreaming in school instead of listening to the teacher? Intense reading, writing, and listening to music are other examples of activities that can put us in a light trance thus altering our attention such that we can become extremely attentive and unconsciously shut off outside subjects vying for our attention. Any activity that intensely focuses your attention is hypnosis.

Furthermore, we sometimes become so affected by the imaginary world of a daydream or a chapter of a book that our emotions take over. We cry over an emotionally meaningful song, feel fear as the villain gets near the hero's hiding place in a story, or even scream over a particularly frightening scene.

This kind of phenomenon, referred to as self-hypnosis, is so common and so human a trait that Milton Erickson, a hypnosis expert in the 20th century and referred to as the father of modern hypnotherapy, concluded that people hypnotise themselves on a daily basis. Hypnosis has aptly been described as "controlled daydreaming."

Note then, that this kind of "everyday trance" is different from the trance brought about by deep hypnosis, and is comparable to that relaxed mental state between wakefulness and sleep. There is also a difference between auto-hypnosis, where the state of extreme suggestibility is self-induced; and hetero-hypnosis, where it is induced by a hypnotist or another person. All these we will try to explain further in the succeeding chapters.

In all of the above-mentioned categories, the hypnotised person, as stated in the Encyclopaedia Britannica, "seems to respond in an uncritical, automatic fashion, ignoring aspects of the environment (e.g., sights, sounds) not pointed out by the hypnotist. Even the subject's memory and awareness of self may be altered by suggestions, and the effects of the suggestions may be extended (post-hypnotically) into the subject's subsequent waking activity…."

In self-induced hypnosis, a person feels relaxed and very open; concerns about the "real world" seem to be forgotten temporarily while buried in a book or engrossed in a film.

This is parallel to hypnosis with the aid of a hypnotist. If the hypnotist states that the subject is in extreme heat, the person may start to sweat and experience high temperature, even if the temperature is perfectly comfortable. If he suggests to a timid and painfully shy person that he is in fact an extremely confident man who is sure of himself, the person may suddenly feel open to socialising with other people, even strangers. Any knowledgeable and experienced hypnotist will be the first to admit that the effect will only be temporary unless the subject truly wants to change.

For example, a person can be made to quit smoking by suggesting through hypnosis that the smoke is poisonous and deadly. That person then starts to become adverse to smoke, and feel nauseous whenever he gets near it. Thus, he may shun cigarettes. But if the person does not truly want to stop smoking, or if he or she is doing it for someone other than him or herself, the habit will probably come back eventually.

Another proven limitation of hypnosis is that a person's common sense, principles, beliefs and life convictions remain unchanged throughout and after the experience. No one can also be hypnotised against their will, because the mind has to be willingly and consciously open to be affected by the hypnotist's suggestions.

For example, hypnosis cannot make a Muslim person eat pork or a Superman fan fly out of a window. Since the mind is still fully alert (only the subconscious is more open) the person's sense of safety is still on guard. His sensibilities will continue to govern his decision-making process.

Then again, we can never really be sure. One story is about a man who was undergoing hypnosis to boost his self-confidence and was told by the hypnotist that he "could do anything, anything as long as he puts his mind into it." For more effect, the hypnotist says: "Why, you could even rob a bank if you want to." Although the hypnotist may have meant the statement only as a metaphor, his subject then proceeds to rob a bank a couple of days later!

There are two points of note here: first, the hypnotist was irresponsible in making such a suggestion even if it was intended as a metaphor, and secondly, the act of robbing a bank was already within the subject's core values, or put another way, the subject's moral compass wasn't working in the first place.

Hypnosis cannot make you do something that you would not otherwise do.

A study says that on the average, 25 out of 100 people can be hypnotised very easily. Almost all children belong to this group, who are perceived to be highly susceptible to suggestion. This ratio varies according to the hypnotist's personality, technique, and experience. The success of the hypnotist also depends on the subject's personality, attention span, and mental status at the moment. Interestingly, while it seems rational that persons with high intellect cannot be easily hypnotised because of their capacity to process all information that gets into their brain, it is in fact the opposite. It is believed that intelligent people are also the most creative, thus they can easily associate the hypnotist's word play with their own visual or sensory representations.

It is those with strong analytical traits that are the most difficult to hypnotise because they never stop analysing what the hypnotist is saying.

It is common to hear someone say, "I can't be hypnotised," and they are absolutely correct. If you think you can or cannot be hypnotised, you are right. It is all up to you.

WORDS OF CAUTION

Hypnosis is a neutral force; it is neither good nor bad. Its value depends on who wields it, and how it will be used. Mind control, the power of suggestion, and tapping into the subconscious, could be dangerous if abused. However, typical hypnosis cannot be used to control other people, but brainwashing can if it is conducted over an extended period of time. Examples of brainwashing include military intelligence operatives and religious cult followers.

Hypnosis has also been linked to creating false memories; therefore, when conducting research such as in alien abductions, past-life regressions, or similar, no hypnotist should ever introduce information during the hypnosis session that the subject has not already offered or stated. This is the same as "leading the subject" and can confabulate the results. Confabulation is the placing of false memories in a subject to fill in a time-gap in memory. This is an absolute no-no in the practice of hypnosis.

Hypnosis is more vulnerable to abuse because it does not take great effort for someone to be able to learn how to do it. Almost anybody can practice it and achieve a minimum of success. And although the effect may be temporary or minimal, still hypnosis has the capacity to alter something in the way the subject may think, behave, or decide in the future.

In this line, caution must especially be taken when dealing with hypnosis. First off, even when handled by a professional, hypnosis is not a cure-all by itself. It is effective if it is used in context, done the right way, and in coordination with other corresponding therapies. It is not a substitute for necessary medical and psychological treatment.

Thus, only a qualified person should attempt to diagnose a person and analyse what affects him or her; and then prescribe an appropriate treatment. The professional will then be able to provide a concise evaluation regarding the case.

Conversely, an unqualified person might misdiagnose the ailment and come up with a wrong or inaccurate interpretation, thus prescribing the wrong course of treatment.

It is best to seek professional medical advice, rather than hypnosis, when the subject is experiencing pain or illness. Not doing so could lead to life-threatening consequences. Pain is the body's way of telling us that something is wrong. Just imagine if you hypnotised the pain away from a person who has a serious disease. If the person you hypnotised did not experience the discomfort brought about by the illness, he would not go to the doctor for a check-up. This could lead to dangerous outcomes and might negatively affect the health and life of that person.

So always be careful when using hypnosis. With power comes responsibility.

HYPNOSIS THROUGHOUT HISTORY

Hypnosis has been known to humans for thousands of years. Historically, the practice of altering a person's consciousness has been carried out by shamans, wiccans, spirit mediums, and spiritual doctors, for various reasons. Ancient civilisations of Egypt and Greece recorded that the fastest way to get in touch with the spiritual realm is through rituals that are similar to what are now called hypnosis, meditation, visualisation, and drugs.

Experiences common to deep sleep, anaesthesia, and the power of the subconscious have been noted in different religious documents, such as in the Old Testament of Christianity and in the Talmud of Judaism.

Some accounts even say that many women were accused as witches and thus burned at the stake because of their practice of "cutting up" women's bellies during difficult labour in order to help the child get out of the womb. It was said the mothers felt relatively no pain during the "operation" and the babies were delivered successfully with the midwives using only herbs and oils while uttering some comforting, soothing chant. This practice, many believed, is one of the earliest known practices of what is now called delivery through Caesarean operation, with the aid of hypnosis.

Taking the cue from their ancient traditions, indigenous cultures even in the present day still benefit from mind control and suggestion and its ability to heal or harm.

MESMERIZING MAGNETISM

In the modern world, hypnosis's first brush with science was known in the late 1700s, through Austrian physician Dr. Franz Anton Mesmer and the "phenomenon" that was called animal magnetism. Mesmer believed that through a mystical force channelled through water tubs and magnetic wands flowing from him to his subjects, he could make people and animals go into trance. He claimed this mystical power was due to magnetic waves. He lulled his subjects into submission through fixating them on a certain object, and through monotonous repetition of certain words. This was where the word "mesmerize" was coined and we still use it today to refer to the act of being in awe or dumbstruck in the presence of a certain figure.

The concept of animal magnetism was eventually dismissed. Abbe Faria, a scientist in the 19th century, declared that the hypnosis practiced by Mesmer was not because of animal magnetism but was through the power of suggestion.

THE PENDULUM

More studies and experiments in mind control followed through the years, but it was research launched in 1842 that was considered the turning point in the study of Mesmer's ideas. Scottish surgeon James Braid was one of the first scientists to attribute the process of going into a trance to a physiological process. He believed that the state of trance was not due to the magnetic power of the hypnotist; but through hard, rapt attention on a striking, moving object over time, as in that iconic clock necklace. "Protracted ocular fixation," Braid believed, will make the brain tired and will cause the subject to be under what he called "nervous sleep." Thus, Braid coined the term "hypnosis" and "hypnotism," based on the Greek word of "sleep."

Braid, with his contemporaries such as Ambroise-Auguste Liebeault, Hippolyte Bernheim and J.M. Charcot, later focused more on the impact of psychological motivation in hypnosis rather that their early concept of fatigue and nervous sleep. They were also the first ones to tread upon medical hypnosis, wherein they used hypnosis to treat different psychological and physical conditions.

Following the paths taken by Braid et al., more studies on the use of hypnosis in medicine followed, with better results this time. Mirroring (though perhaps unconsciously) the practices of ancient doctors, modern medicine started to cautiously tread upon the use of hypnosis as anaesthesia or pain killers. The medicine world then had a strong disbelief in this method; as in a case in 1842, when there was a report of a successful and painless amputation procedure through hypnosis. But it was quickly dismissed.

Still, pro-hypnosis medical professionals persisted with their studies. Dr. James Esdaile, a British physician who practiced in India, performed almost 400 pain-controlled operations with patients under hypnosis. Known as the "Father of Hypno-Anaesthesia," Esdaile also integrated his Western education with the culture in India. Hand-in hand with his medical practice, he also performed a drugless trance therapy traditionally from Bengal, India. Esdaile's cases listed eye, ear, and throat operations, amputations, and tumours and cancerous growth removals. Esdaile reported no pain and zero mortality under his so-called "mental anaesthesia."

What's more astonishing is that after the surgeries, Esdaile further hypnotically suggested to his patients that their wounds would not result in any kind of infection or side effect. True enough, no one among his patients was reported to have caught any post-operation side effects. Many believed the subconscious aspects of Esdaile's subjects responded well to hypnosis.

When Esdaile suggested they would not be infected, their bodily functions acted accordingly and launched antibodies that would fight infection.

Because of the deaths of Braid, Esdaile, and other kindred colleagues plus the advancement of anaesthetics though chemicals, the interest in hypnosis waned.

HYPNOTICALLY HYSTERICAL

Hysteria and hypnosis? Strange bedfellows at first glance maybe; but after hypnosis kept a relatively low profile after the death of Braid, hypnosis made a comeback in the 1880s as new versions of his work were circulated. The revival also came with new experimentations, particularly in the use of hypnosis in treating hysteria led by neurologist Jean Martin Charcot.

The dictionary defines "hysteria" as "a psychoneurotic disorder characterised by violent emotional outbreaks, disturbances of sensory and motor functions, and various abnormal effects due to autosuggestion."

Charcot, and later his pupil Pierre Janet, treated various cases of mental conditions, but most particularly hysteria, through what they called *dissociation*. Hypnosis, utilised with a large number of patients, compartmentalises some of the data stored in the mind, so that aspects such as a particular skill or information from the past can be hidden or retrieved.

Considered landmark experiments at that time, these findings impressed and inspired later works of French psychologist Alfred Biet and the father of psychoanalysis Sigmund Freud.

In fact, Freud used the works of Charcot and another French doctor, Hippolyte Bernheim, to strengthen the framework of his initial studies on the unconscious and hypnosis.

Meanwhile, science has enriched the layman's dictionary once again since it was in this time that Ambroise-Auguste Liebeault coined the term *rapport* meaning that critical and required affinity between the hypnotist and the subject for a successful hypnosis session. Today, we still use the word rapport to mean that pleasant connection and affinity between two parties; a certain similarity in wavelength.

HYPNOSIS AND WAR

A powerful weapon, a strategic device, an intelligence technique, and a medical tool—all these roles were said to have been taken by hypnosis during World Wars I and II.

War trauma is common to soldiers who have faced the horrors of war.

Hypnosis was used by physicians to help patients in letting go of their repressed memories, and to eventually treat amnesia or other resulting conditions. This kind of therapy also helps the patient to alleviate emotional and mental tensions resulting from the trauma. The powerful suggestions invoked by hypnosis were also used as a tool for military intelligence. For example, extremely confidential information that has to be passed personally can be protected through the power of suggestion. In this case, the information will be given to a soldier under hypnosis. After the information has been relayed successfully, the hypnotist then suggests to the courier that he will never remember a single detail about the message, thus ensuring that it remains a secret forever.

Since hypnosis can also be effective in altering the behaviour of a person, it was used as a strategy to infiltrate the enemy's ranks. G.H. Estabrooks, a physician who worked with United States Authorities in World War II, divulged in a medical journal that the behaviour modification properties of hypnosis were useful in sending a deep penetration agent inside a communist territory. He also stated:

"I worked this technique with a vulnerable Marine lieutenant I'll call "Jones." Under the watchful eye of Marine Intelligence, I spilt his personality into Jones A and Jones B. Jones A, once a "normal" working Marine, became entirely different. He talked communist doctrine and meant it. He was welcomed enthusiastically by communist cells, was deliberately given a dishonourable discharge by the Corps (which was in on the plot) and became a card-carrying party member."

What Estabrooks describes above is now known as "Parts Therapy" and has been used to positively treat other issues that don't involve the spy world.

HYPNOTIC REGRESSIONS

Hypnosis may not make you younger, but it can make you feel and act younger. It may not take away pain, but it may fool around with your pain sensors so that pain may virtually be non-existent. For all the fallacies and myths surrounding hypnosis, there are still a number of things hypnosis can do that are beneficial and scientifically proven. In general medicine, psychology, surgery, and dentistry, and even in the legal system, hypnosis has been known to help people gain better understanding of the situation and themselves.

AGE REGRESSION

Wise men have said: "Those who do not remember history are condemned to repeat it. Whatever you are now, the skills you possess, the ailments that bother you, may have something to do with your past."

In regression, the person that initiates your hypnosis dips into a particular period in your life, for example, when you were still in nursery school. This suggestion triggers you to live out significant incidents in that period. Since you are "re-living the past," you may think, talk, or act as you did in nursery school.

Your hypnotist and you can then determine how a particular incident in that period may be connected with a condition affecting you presently. Reliving a part of your past may help you recover some vital information, establish insights, or aid you to know yourself better and how to cope with the present.

TOOL FOR SURGERY

Painless surgery and dentistry have been proven to be possible with just the help of hypnosis. Mothers about to give birth, soldiers wounded in the midst of a battle, or children nervous of a tooth extraction have all benefited from hypnosis as an anaesthetic.

During the operation, the hypnotised patient is reported to have remained relaxed and at ease. Post-surgery hypnosis is also known to aid in prevention of infection or to relieve discomfort and pain. Increased recovery speed is also a known benefit of hypnosis.

BEHAVIOUR MODIFICATION

Making someone act like a chicken is only icing on hypnosis' cake. There are other pleasant and useful cases wherein its ability to modify behaviour is vital.

On a long–term basis, hypnosis can be used as a central part of treating psychological conditions such as anxiety, depression, trauma, or phobias.

Therapy with the aid of hypnosis is also useful in curbing habits such as smoking, drugs, eating disorders, or social anxiety.

TREATING PHYSICAL PROBLEMS DUE TO PSYCHOLOGICAL FACTORS

Many of our physical problems are linked with our psychological condition, given the direct link of the brain and the nervous system to the separate processes of other parts of the body. That's why some doctors believe there is no other way to treat a physical condition more efficiently than to go directly to the brain.

Psycho-physiological conditions are ailments of the body that can be rooted from psychological factors. Usually, a person vulnerable to a certain illness, when faced with stress, will likely catch a psychosomatic illness. A medical definition usually states that a psychosomatic illness is a condition in which the state of mind (psyche) either causes or mediates a condition of actual, measurable damage in the body (soma).

Columbia Encyclopaedia further notes a psychosomatic disorder as an "emotional disturbance that is manifested as a physical disorder," such as childhood asthma, ulcers, hypertension, endocrine disturbances, and possibly even heart disease. In most cases the illness occurs only when both physiological predisposition and psychological stress are present. In this formula, predisposition pertains to your mental and medical history.

Stress concerns with elements that make you feel anxious or bothered, as well as outside stimuli such as problems in the family or society eventually triggers the onset of illness. These include death, conflicts (personal or social), emotional problems, and financial worries.

Other conditions that result from psychological stress are problems that affect vital organs: the heart, stomach, lungs, liver and the nervous system, triggering the onset of cancer, stroke, arthritis, multiple sclerosis and pain.

A typical script when using hypnosis to aid in the treatment of psychosomatic illnesses is similar to other hypnosis scripts that aim at changing or asserting a certain condition. First, the hypnotist guides the subject into deep relaxation until the body and mind are completely at ease. The subject is then encouraged to imagine each and every part of his personality that is ailing, physically and mentally.

Using visual imagery that promotes wellbeing and lightness, the hypnotist tells the patient to ease away his pain, anxiety, and other thoughts that bother him.

The hypnotist may also identify each body part, giving particular importance to the affected ones, and thus helps the patient handle, overcome, or come to terms with the pain.

USES IN THE LEGAL SYSTEM

The mind's capacity to store information is astounding. It can even act like a video camera that zooms in, pauses, fast forwards or slows down a certain event. The problem is, we tend to "forget" because, however big its capacity, it is not limitless; it compartmentalises and organises memory so it can accommodate more. This is where hypnosis comes in. Hypnosis can help a person retrieve relevant information that may have been discarded or neglected in normal everyday activities. Pinpointing critical data is especially important in solving crime cases. Hypnosis has been used to help witnesses and victims of crime sort out information from the crime scene. By intensely focusing through hypnosis on memories relating to the crime, a significant detail, a vital clue, or an element previously forgotten may aid in the investigation.

Still, police do not usually rely heavily on hypnosis in solving crimes. The mind is tricky, and people can be tricky too. As we said before, people under hypnosis can still decide for themselves. People under hypnosis may lie, or prefer not to divulge a secret. As previously stated, whoever you are normally is who you will be in hypnosis. If you are honest in normal life, you'll be honest in hypnosis.

STAGE HYPNOSIS

Like any other thing in contemporary age, hypnosis has not escaped the glitter, glamour, and kitsch of commercialism. It's not really surprising that something as mysterious and as interesting as hypnosis can turn into an entertainment show for moneymaking ventures.

Still, this is not to say that stage hypnotists are not as genuine as their counterparts in the clinical setting. Professional stage hypnotists follow the same rules and techniques in hypnosis as clinicians. They just tweak them to provide entertainment value. The effect of their brand of hypnosis to their subjects doesn't differ either; people act silly or ridiculous because it's their will to go along with the show. As one stage hypnotist puts it, volunteer subjects act and behave the way they think hypnotised people act and behave.

So, you want to be a Blackpool show hypnotist? Perfect timing, right pacing, and action-packed sequences are some of the required elements in a truly entertaining show. Here are some tips compiled from professionals of the trade.

COLLECT AND SELECT

Almost all stage hypnotists initiate a pre-selection process prior to the show. These are not "planted" talents; the hypnotist actually calls out for volunteers from the current audience. After a series of hypnosis exercises, the hypnotist determines who among them is the most suggestible to hypnosis. For every level, he selects the highly suggestible ones and eliminates those he deems not ready or not open to "let go." (Thank you very much sir, ma'am, you may take your seat now.) This ensures a faster pace of the show, a more successful hypnosis rate; therefore, a more entertaining show. The hypnotist performs hypnosis exercises at different levels.

TWELVE MINUTES OF FAME

People, more or less, are attracted to the lure of the spotlight, if not confused by it. Putting people on stage in front of a large audience increases the success rate of the hypnosis session. On stage, people find it hard to resist hypnotic instructions compared to common situations and feel "obliged" to behave as they are expected to. Thus, they find it easy to follow and respond to the hypnotist's suggestions so as not to ruin the show. Once the atmosphere comes to this, the participants start to loosen up. The audience buys the act accordingly. This is enough for the hypnotist to take advantage of. All he has to do now, is "direct" the show. Cooperation is much easier if it's all part of a performance.

WASH THEIR HANDS CLEAN

Riding on the idea that hypnotised people have absolutely no idea or control to what they are doing, subjects may find it easier to act out what is asked of them, no matter how weird or silly it may be. Once hypnotised, one may believe (or the hypnotist suggests one to believe) that he has no responsibility for the volunteer's actions. It's not "really them" who are acting like ducks and quacking on stage. Somebody is making them do what might have been embarrassing things.

SHOWMANSHIP

Bring out that fog machine! Turn on those bright lights! Let those glitters pour on! Don't shy away from sound effects. Music for more ambience! Costumes and props for more atmosphere!

Once the show achieves the aura of a cinema house, the audience, in automatic response akin to that of a moviegoer, will be ready to suspend their disbelief. They will believe everything that is being fed to them from the stage. As in a fantastical and magical film, however irrational the story twist may be, the audience is ready and willing to buy in.

Almost all stage hypnotists use stage tricks in order to achieve more jaw-dropping impact. The more complicated and dangerous the stage acrobatics are the better for them (and their ticket sales). One common impressive stunt is suspending a person between two chairs, and then letting somebody stand on that person's chest. The audience doesn't question the trick; but in reality it's just an ingenious use of space, black cloth, mirrors, and yes, hypnosis.

Make 'Em Wet Their Pants

Talk in a booming, authoritative voice. Astound the audience and the participants with your commanding stance. The stage hypnotist takes advantage of the participant's excitement, nervousness, and inexperience on the stage. He taps into that social pressure placed upon the subject. If others look as if they are under the hypnotist's control, they must be. He also takes into consideration that people act according to what they deem appropriate, after all, if this is a hypnosis show then they have to go with the flow. Never let them question your authority. Understand that hypnotised subjects may still wield their own free will, but generally people do what they are told, more so if it's from an imposing figure.

At the same time, an ethical, professional hypnotist never exploits the participant's vulnerability. He respects the subject's sense of self and dignity. He puts importance on their safety and well-being. Being the performer that he is, the stage hypnotist tries his best to give the audience and the participants a great time.

We build our reputation on your success

OUR UNIQUE APPROACH TO TEACHING

Here at Innervisions School of Clinical Hypnosis, we stand apart from other training providers by offering an approach that goes beyond the traditional methods of clinical hypnosis education.

Our philosophy is centred around bringing to our students the most current, in-demand topics, techniques, and tools that reflect the latest advancements in the field.

But it's not just about what we teach; it's about how we teach it.

Our goal is to empower our students to work intuitively, to trust in their own abilities, and to develop the confidence needed to be authentic and successful in their practice.

We believe that true mastery comes from within, and we foster an environment where every student feels supported and capable of achieving their best.

Our training isn't just about delivering information; it's about transformation.

We boost our students' self-esteem and confidence, ensuring that when they step into their roles as therapists, they do so with a deep sense of authenticity and trust in their unique authentic style.

We don't believe in a one-size-fits-all approach to therapy, and neither should our students. That's why we provide a therapeutic toolbox that is second to none. Filled with flexible, adaptable techniques that can be mixed, matched, and customized for each individual client. Every client is unique, and we ensure that our students are fully equipped to create bespoke therapeutic interventions that are tailored to their clients' specific needs.

We build our reputation on your success

The thing that truly sets us apart is our nurturing, caring approach to teaching.

We are deeply committed to our students' success, and that commitment is reflected in the way we deliver our training.

We bring you cutting-edge techniques and tools rooted in the latest research, ensuring you are always on the forefront of the field. But more than that, we create a learning environment where you will feel supported, inspired, and ready to excel.

At Innervisions School of Clinical Hypnosis, we believe in your potential, and we give you everything you need to realise it.

This combination of support, authenticity, and innovation is what makes us stand head and shoulders above the rest.

"We build our reputation...

      On your success..."

OUR VIRTUAL CLASSROOM

Having spent over 25 years teaching live in venues across the UK, we were pleasantly surprised when we were forced into using a virtual classroom during the Covid 'lockdown'.

We pioneered a system that works even better than face to face classroom training by utilising the internationally renowned Zoom platform. We use breakout room facilities where you can practice one to one, supervised by our world class tutors.

We have found that even so called 'technophobes' soon get used to using this virtual classroom and embrace the numerous advantages of such.

Here are just some of the many benefits in training via our Live Virtual Classroom

- ✓ Learn from home
- ✓ No issue with inclement weather
- ✓ No dependency on public transport
- ✓ No need for childcare or animal sitters
- ✓ Save money (food, travel)
- ✓ No dependency on venues
- ✓ Reduced time commitment
- ✓ No travelling to venues
- ✓ Zero risk of cross viral infections
- ✓ Accelerated learning environment
- ✓ More breaks
- ✓ More focus
- ✓ Less distractions
- ✓ Successful mode of teaching and therapy.

POST TRAINING

Post training, we have a unique and large hypnotherapy support community group; all graduates will be added to this page post training.

Also, we have a unique one to one and/or peer group supervision service for all our graduates via zoom on a monthly basis. Details and dates are posted in our private community group.

Furthermore, post training we offer our own in house exclusive CPD classes on various subjects which are also promoted in our private community group.

REFRESHER VIDEOS

We provide video tutorials of Modules One to Five with links to other videos and demonstrations.

These videos are for the sole use of past and present Innervisions students, and public distribution of any of the access links is strictly prohibited. Any breach of this condition will result in immediate expulsion from any further training and notification to GHSC.

In order to access the videos, please go on line to our website where you will find access to the modules after they are covered in class. www.innervisions.co.uk

Each module is password protected.

HYPNOTHERAPY AS A CAREER

1. HIGH CAREER SATISFACTION

According to Career Explorer, hypnotherapists are ranked in the top 15% of professionals when it comes to career satisfaction. The primary reason is that an overwhelming majority of hypnotherapists find their work meaningful.

In fact, being a hypnotherapist helps you effectively address a wealth of issues that may have been bothering people for a significant period of time, such as long-term trauma, and if that's not satisfying, we don't know what else is. Who doesn't like the client saying, "You have changed my life for the better"? As a hypnotherapist, you will get to hear that, and similar positive feedback, a lot if you treat your clients right.

Not only that, but if you have good training and become a professional hypnotherapist, you will have the knowledge and skills to work with people who have new and unique problems, which means you will develop from working with each new challenge and get a chance to hone your skills and further enhance your change work abilities.

Besides that, a hypnotherapist has plenty of opportunities for career development, proper work-life balance, and decent job security. All these factors contribute to high job satisfaction. With such high career satisfaction, why look for any other career option?

2. A CAREER WHERE IT IS EASY TO BE SELF-EMPLOYED

According to the National Careers Service (NCS), the majority of hypnotherapists are self-employed. That hypnotherapy is recognised by the NCS indicates that it is an acceptable business mode.

Being a self-employed professional certainly brings with it many perks like:

- You are in charge of how much you want to charge your clients
- You decide when to work, so you have more flexibility in working hours
- If you want to work as a part-time hypnotherapist, or term-time only, or alongside another job, it's possible.

You can also set up your practice in whichever city or town you prefer; that certainly reduces the need to relocate and the resultant expenses.

Very few other career options provide you with so much freedom.

3. A CAREER WITH SUPERIOR EARNINGS

By now, you might think, all that is great, but what about the money?

Let us tell you the average hourly rate of a hypnotherapist is higher than that of a data scientist and machine learning engineer (both of these skills are in great demand). As per Payscale, the average hourly pay for a hypnotherapist in the UK is £60.68. The base rate is usually £50. Yet if you work in a city, the fee may be significantly higher. For example, hypnotherapists in London, UK commonly charge £90 – £250 per hour.

Hypnotherapy is a brief, strategic therapy. As such, treatment often lasts for 6-12 sessions, depending on the client's issues and their goals. Therefore, the average earning per client is significant, which makes this career even more lucrative.

Also, since most hypnotherapists are self-employed, you will be responsible for setting the session rates. That's why, after gaining some experience, hypnotherapists often reflect their abilities in their rates, which allows you to make an above-average income even with a limited set of clients.

4. A CAREER WITH FLEXIBILITY WITHIN YOUR WORKING HOURS

The job of a hypnotherapist is cognitively demanding. Rather than just listen whilst someone complains about their life for an hour, you are actively engaging with the client to explore and generate change. That's why you benefit from scheduling the sessions when you are most attentive. Being self employed, you can decide on when you will be seeing clients, the duration and location of the sessions, and when you will be engaged in your office tasks, such as marketing and website work.

According to The Institute of Applied Psychology, a good hypnotherapist conducts sessions only for 20 hours weekly. Sure enough, you need to consistently develop your business in the remaining time and even market your service, but attending to clients is a percentage of your overall time.

As for the associated tasks like marketing, you can always outsource them if you prefer. With the career not being demanding in terms of time, it's easy to have a proper work-life balance.

5. A CAREER WITH A WORK-FROM-HOME OPTION AVAILABLE

As a hypnotherapist, you can work from the venue of your choice. The three options you mostly like have are:

Therapy setting (e.g. clinic):Working from a clinic or talking therapy centre is, of course, the most obvious one. However, that means you might have to spend money to lease a room. Saying that, some places allow you to book by the hour.

Work from home: Working from home is another great option. That way, you can save time because you won't have to commute. Similarly, you will save money on room hire. Although, you will either be dedicating the sole use of a room at home, or find a way to make a room dual purpose (e.g., living room / client room).

Online: Did you know you can conduct hypnotherapy sessions online as well? This means that you can travel anywhere in the world and as long as there is an internet connection, you are still able to work with your clients.

Ultimately, as a professional hypnotherapist, you will have complete freedom over the venue and medium you want to provide the sessions. Almost no other profession provides you with such freedom. Freedom to work from anywhere is another reason to become a hypnotherapist.

6. A CAREER WHICH GIVES YOU THE ABILITY TO HELP VAST ARRAY OF CLIENTS

When someone hears the word hypnotherapy they often associate it with smoking cessation, weight management, relieving trauma, or past life regression therapy. However, a hypnotherapist works with a wide array of people, such as:

- ✓ Athletes
- ✓ Business people
- ✓ Children
- ✓ Groups
- ✓ Housewives/ husbands
- ✓ Parents / grandparents
- ✓ and so on.

A hypnotherapist can help with changes to the mind and the body, thus both psychological issues, and physiological issues. It means anyone who has a fear of public speaking, stuttering, low self-esteem, and so on will benefit from going to a hypnotherapist.

7. A CAREER WITHOUT MONOTONY

The job of a hypnotherapist is a challenging one. As highlighted above, as a professional hypnotherapist, you can help clients with a slew of problems. Even if you usually get clients experiencing similar problems, such as, for example, anxiety, the cause of that anxiety, and the contributory factors can be different each time.

As a hypnotherapist, you have to first find out about the client's problem, how it affects them and also what they want to achieve. Thereafter, together with the client you will decide on the most effective course of treatment. You may have 10 clients with anxiety, but each will have different causes, contributory factors and goals.

The point we are making is, as a hypnotherapist, no two clients are the same. That certainly makes the job more challenging.

Unlike some other career options, your skills are challenged every day to provide the best possible solution to your clients. That certainly eliminates monotony.

8. A CAREER WITH ENDLESS OPPORTUNITIES

To understand the slew of opportunities, it's important to understand the growth of the Complementary and Alternative Medicine market first. According to a market analysis report, this segment is expected to grow at 25.1% from 2023 to 2030 in the USA. Similar growth is expected globally.

Apart from that, studies are being conducted globally which highlight the effectiveness of hypnotherapy in tackling various significant health issues affecting groups of society. For example, a recent study concluded that hypnotherapy is a promising way to help obese people lose weight.

In another example, many sports teams, like the Swiss ski team and the US White Sox baseball team, have hired a full-time hypnotherapist to help athletes extract their full potential.

Similarly, Kate Middleton used Hypnobirthing.

It means the applications of hypnotherapy are increasing swiftly. That certainly indicates the rise in opportunities. The greater the number of uses of hypnotherapy, the wider your client base becomes.

9. A CAREER WHICH MEETS A HIGH DEMAND

According to data collected by Find Courses, the salary of a hypnotherapist has been on an upward trend for the last five years. Such an earnings trend can only be sustained if there is a high demand for hypnotherapists.

So, when you become a professional hypnotherapist, you are learning a skill in high demand, which is likely to provide year-on-year growth.

10. A CAREER THAT CAN BE COMPLIMENTARY TO YOUR PRIMARY OCCUPATION

Most other careers that pay equally well, require you to devote all of your available time or work full time. However, you won't face this problem with hypnotherapy. There are numerous reasons why hypnotherapy can be a good complementary career:

Since most hypnotherapists are self-employed, choosing your working hours is easy. That means your primary occupation isn't at risk.

After becoming a hypnotherapist, one can also teach others, which is an even less demanding job.

It means there are numerous reasons why hypnotherapy is a suitable second career.

11. A HYPNOTHERAPY CAREER WHERE YOU CAN OFFER FAST TREATMENT

For a rapid solution to a tension headache, many people will reach for a tablet. The same for many other conditions. Yet pills can stop you addressing the cause, and can enable you to suppress many emotions and symptoms. On the other hand, hypnotherapy can help you explore the root causes.

When comparing the effectiveness and speed of hypnotherapy, compare it with other talking therapies rather than medicine. When you do that, you will realize that hypnotherapy requires fewer sessions, compared to talking therapies.

You might be thinking, why so? Talking therapies communicate with your conscious mind. Hypnotherapy, in most cases, communicates with the entire person, including their conscious and subconscious mind. Sometimes a client may struggle with their ability to understand and analyse the world from their perspective. Yet if their perceptions are distorted, they will find it difficult to relate to certain situations and may also not be able to alter unhelpful patterns or thoughts. Hypnotherapy enables people to more easily and effectively identify obstacles to change, and find solutions.

So, what better way to help people than opting for a faster form of therapy?

12. A CAREER WITH THE FREEDOM TO BE CREATIVE

Most people who aren't familiar with hypnotherapy think that there is only 1 technique in it. That involves putting the patient in a hypnotic trance and telling them what to do. That's wrong! Hypnotherapy is much more than that. Different techniques that a hypnotherapist can use include:

- ✓ Anaesthesia and analgesia techniques – for pain management
- ✓ Analytical approaches to gain insight
- ✓ Behavioural approaches to identify and change habits and responses
- ✓ Cognitive approaches to identify and change distorted and rigid beliefs and thoughts
- ✓ Ego strengthening – to boost self-esteem and increase resilience
- ✓ Mental rehearsal and future pacing – to explore potential responses and practice chosen actions
- ✓ Metaphors – to enable the client to choose their own responses
- ✓ Regression approaches to revisit the past to optimise resources and gain new perspectives
- ✓ Suggestions – direct (tell) and indirect (invite) suggestions, bespoke to the specific needs of the client
- ✓ Time distortion – to alter the perception of time passing

A hypnotherapist can use one or multiple techniques to achieve the desired results for a client. Since each case is different, it's up to the hypnotherapist to decide which methods to use and agree the treatment approach with the client. Thus, a hypnotherapist has complete freedom to practice his/her craft.

13. A CAREER WITH CONSISTENT LEARNING

Many careers might seem exciting at the start, but once you practice the career for a couple of years, you realize nothing new is involved. Soon enough, the career seems like a burden. With hypnotherapy, you won't suffer from this problem.

Wondering why so? Because the field of hypnotherapy is evolving consistently. Not only are the applications increasing, but also the techniques that can be used.

Moreover, according to the General Hypnotherapy Standards Council, professional hypnotherapists must complete 15 hours of Continuing Professional Development (CPD) learning each year to remain registered. As a hypnotherapist, you will consistently evolve your skills, and therefore, there will never be a dull moment.

14. A CAREER WITH OPTIONS TO SPECIALISE

Want to earn more as a hypnotherapist? Opting for a specialisation! It helps you stand out from the competition, charge more, and optimise niche opportunities. Wondering which are the specialization opportunities? Some options include:

- ✓ Anxiety
- ✓ Assertiveness
- ✓ Bereavement and loss
- ✓ Conception and childhood (bed-wetting, childhood anxiety disorders, pregnancy, psychogenic infertility)
- ✓ Confidence
- ✓ Dental hypnosis
- ✓ IBS
- ✓ Insomnia
- ✓ Memory enhancement
- ✓ Pain management
- ✓ Performance anxiety
- ✓ Phobias and phobic disorders
- ✓ Smoking cessation
- ✓ Snoring
- ✓ Sport hypnosis
- ✓ Stress management
- ✓ Weight management (weight loss and weight gain)

With so many opportunities available, a clear career progression path is available.

15. A CAREER WITH THE ABILITY TO DO SOMETHING FOR THE SOCIETY

If you are looking for a higher purpose to become a hypnotherapist, you can always give away your services for free or help raise money for a charity of your choice. Since hypnotherapists are in great demand, it's not that difficult to give back to society.

Not only that, you can provide them in remote areas online or even by visiting those places, which allows you to do something for people who are in dire need of your services but don't have the resources to travel to larger cities.

WHAT THE PEOPLE SAY:

We have built our reputation over the years based on the success of our students.

Our policy of transparency and compassion are vitally important to us as is our dedication to ensure that every single student is trained to the highest of standards.

When we asked our graduates on our dedicated Facebook group page to send us their views on the quality of our training and their own unique story of their journey to success, we were inundated with totally unbiased and honest reviews, some of which follow on the proceeding pages.

We are delighted and proud to introduce you to some of the best hypnotherapists in the whole of Europe all trained to world class standards by Innervisions School of Clinical Hypnosis.

KAREN TAYLOR: HYPNOTHERAPY ECKINGTON

I decided to train as a hypnotherapist after working as a nursery nurse for many years as well as in the community with clients and their families who needed help because they had terminal illness.

My husband passed away with a terminal illness and after several years of working in the community I decided I wanted to try a different career path as my health was suffering. I'd always had an interest in way you do things automatically and how the Brain works and functions and I'd gained lots of qualifications in psychology and emotional behavior and development whilst working with children.

After the free weekend I totally knew actually on day one the course was for me. Module one was amazing lots of practical demonstrations, videos with actual hypnotherapy sessions and comprehensive course notes. The group was friendly, lovely like minded people and we learnt so much and practiced virtually straight away. I enjoyed it and was so excited and amazed at how the techniques worked.

Any questions we had were answered by the tutor and he even helped me with some pain I was experiencing in my hip. I was so amazed by the power of hypnosis I knew this was my career path.

The course lasted 10 months. Every month we learnt so much. We were encouraged around half way though the course to practice our skills and charge a training rate which I did and I started to build up my confidence and client base with the support of the tutor who was always there to answer questions and supervise our progress. My confidence was soaring after even the first weekend.

We were given tasks throughout the course to complete. I always felt fully supported throughout all of the course and in between the monthly weekends the tutor was available to answer questions though a private group if needed.

After qualifying the support goes on though Innervisions family. There is a group for Innervisions practitioners were you can discuss issues with tutors other hypnotherapists who have all trained with this amazing school. Monthly supervision is also available, CPD with lots of interesting specialised courses and skill improvement. Working alone when you've qualified and running your own business never feels like your alone the support whether it's business advice, advice with clients, technology or anything else there is always help available. I set up my hypnotherapy practice, From the heart hypnosis and spiritual services virtually straight away after qualifying, Innervisions gave me the confidence and knowledge to do this.

LAURA CALLAGHAN: HYPNOTHERAPY BY LAURA CALLAGHAN

My road to Hypnotherapy was a very serendipitous one as if often the case. I was struggling with Post Natal Depression after the birth of my son. Counselling sent me in the direction of a past passion for yoga and it was there I discovered a hypnotherapist who inspired me.

I signed up for the Innervisions free weekend that same day. Before Hypnotherapy I worked in Events, the arts and education plus travelled... a bit of a free spirit. I had never even considered doing anything holistic before that but I think it happened at the right time of my life.

I had no idea what to expect when I attended module one that weekend in Leeds. I was really open minded and had it in my head that I was going to do this... this was the next chapter in my life. I loved that weekend, I remember practicing and thinking that it wasn't going to be as easy as I had thought it would be. It was a really informative weekend, the people I met were lovely and I still have close friends today from that weekend plus my tutor was amazing. I came away with so much new knowledge and felt like my brain was brimming over.

My tutor was fantastic and so very knowledgeable. She inspired me but also made me wonder if I could ever be as good as her. I anticipated the weekends every month excitedly and learned so very much. I began practicing on family and colleagues. That is one of the most important things I think, to practice straight away and get out there to hone your skills. There were elements of the course I enjoyed more than others, but it was fantastic overall.

It was disappointing that COVID happened in the middle of our course but it couldn't be helped and the online learning via zoom was fine. Just a shame we didn't get to celebrate at the end in the same way. The gap in the middle of my training gave me the opportunity to carry on practicing.

Post training support is fantastic. There is an absolute wealth of knowledge and helpful materials available on the Innervisions Facebook group page. You don't feel like you're alone, which you essentially are when you qualify. The other therapists in the Facebook group become your colleagues and there is no problem that they won't help you with.

There are many CPD courses that you can attend - Parts Therapy, EFT, law of attraction amongst others plus monthly supervisions and regular nuggets of wisdom in video form from Brian. Innervisions is constantly shifting and changing so you're kept abreast of everything.

There is also a lot of online support from GHR and other bodies if required. The important thing to know is that if you're ever feeling like you're alone after qualifying, just put yourself out there on the group and you'll quickly realise you're not... other therapists always offer to help and do Zoom calls with you etc.

We build our reputation on your success

My hypnotherapy practice has grown over the past two years. I had a goal at the beginning and I'm on track with it.
I began practicing on paying clients in May 2020 and since then I see on average three clients per week, sometimes more sometimes less.

This is fantastic for me as I also work part time for the Police. I run a small practice, but it gives me time to concentrate on the clients I do see and work towards growing my practice when my son goes to school.

Hypnotherapy has led me down a path I never expected and opened up so many doors for me in terms of personal development and better mental health. For the first time in my life I feel balanced and in touch with my unconscious mind to better be able to understand myself and find a peaceful tranquil state.#

I have learnt so many new techniques, many of which I practice on myself daily so that they almost become part of a daily routine for wellness. This has also given me a confidence which I never possessed before I started on this journey.

JAYNE PADLEY: J E CLINICAL HYPNOTHERAPY

In 2018 I had decided to plan for my retirement from nursing which I had been doing since 1983. I set out some achievable goals and planned this I studied specialist counselling diploma NLP practitioner and life coaching but I also sold my house which enabled me to pay for hypnotherapy course as I had looked into this but needed the funds. By doing all this I was investing in myself. I knew that I still wanted to offer support to people as I am both caring and compassionate. I am also only young to retire so still want to work but do something different.

Module one was unusual for me it was in the middle of covid and via zoom but still looked forward to meeting new people and the experience. I felt that to get the best out of the module and course I would put all my previous training to one side and absorb with fresh eyes all that I was being taught. I was totally hooked from the beginning thanks to the tutor and the way the course was presented. Everything was explained and demonstrated so easily and with me being open to all of this it ensured that I was free to take to the study.

The tutor was amazing very knowledgeable about the programme and had her own practice so she could draw on her own experiences and skills to educate us in the history tools and techniques also responsibilities and regulations that would be needed to be a hypnotherapist. The course was divided up into modules and could be paid for prior to each one but we had four weeks between each module to practice and do any work to be handed in which was good for me as I was still a full time nurse but it was more than manageable.

Before the course even finished the support was available and we were given all the information to help with our business our registration and development. There are monthly supervision topics which are great for Continual Professional Development (CPD) and Innervisions community for advice and support so definitely do not feel alone.

As I trained via zoom, my practice is via zoom. it is only small, and like i said at the beginning I planned for retirement so I manage my time. I focused on weight control to begin with but I am now getting clients for fears, phobias, motivation, chronic pain, confidence and so I am getting to fully utilize the tools and skills I have been taught. I only take on about 3 clients per week, that's all I need to make my living.

NICKI CLARKE: NICKI CLARK HYPNOTHERAPY

My story goes back to 1996 when I started my hypnotic journey with Innervisions School Of Clinical Hypnosis. Brian had hair then and he was my tutor 😊

I had a difficult childhood and watched my family suffer incredible trauma through a tragic accident which resulted in death.

Depression, Anxiety and addictions formed within my direct family and I was unable to help them. I buried my hand and concentrated on working full time to support my family financially and study my degree part time at Liverpool John Moore's University.

Years later I heard about a technique called hypnotherapy and loved the idea of being able to assist people through trauma without living through trauma. I worked in sales at the time so I figured that my personality would be useful in gaining rapport when I decided to pursue this dream of being able to help others. Attending this course was the best decision I ever made in my life.

We build our reputation on your success

I was extremely nervous about attending, I have worked from being 15 years old in retail, sales and manufacturing. The idea of being hypnotised was terrifying yet exciting but the idea of learning a skill that literally could change the way people felt or reacted was just too good to miss.

Any doubt or fear was eradicated within the first hour, I realised the people I was sat with were feeling exactly the same and the tutors were fantastic. Within the first weekend, I had learned how to hypnotise someone and experienced the wonderful feeling of hypnosis for myself.

25 years later, I'm still using the skills acquired and I am still often astounded by the results even now.

Even all those years ago, course was easy to follow and well written. The homework was interesting and practical and the encouragement to buddy up and practise with your peers was welcomed. There was just enough time between each module to allow you to practise and give you the confidence to develop your skills further

The knowledge, skills and experience of the tutor were incredible.

Brian was empathic, interesting and extremely supportive in every aspect of the learning. I can honestly say in 25 years, this course is one of the best courses I have ever taken and remains one of the most exciting, rewarding and useful courses I have ever taken.

As I studied with Innervisions 25 years ago, many changes within the course structure, facilities and support have occurred and Innervisions have evolved into a world wide leader in training. At the time you were given as much after support as required and each student was issued with all the modules and the relevant scripts.

After several years I re established contact with Innervisions and immediately without question they gave me access to all resources -

something that I personally find particularly impressive - the material you are issued is incredible, the support outstanding and the access easy to manage. The team of tutors are readily available to provide any support needed and often give you more than expected and the group are familiar, friendly and supportive at all times. It's a pleasure to be in this community and I'm grateful for having found Innervisions.

I run my practise part time and focus on working with people suffering from stress, anxiety and depression. More recently I have been working with teenagers who have attended counselling and achieved minimal results. Within 2 sessions they feel like they have got their lives back and their parents are delighted. I have never had a smoker fail to stop smoking and I have worked with most phobias.

The pleasure you get from actually helping someone to improve their lives is intangible, giving them the power back never stops being amazing, being a clinical hypnotherapist is the most rewarding job in the world and I'm privileged to be a part of it.

KAREN GOODWIN: BEAUTIFUL MINDS

I had been in the hair and beauty field of work for over forty years. Within that time I had also trained in many genres of holistic therapy, including meditation. I've always been interested in the mind as I, like many people have experienced things in my life which have impacted on myself in different ways. I have been running a meditation class for a few years now, where I would take members of the class into visualisations to help them clear blocks and find peace and relaxation.

A friend of mine suggested that perhaps I would find hypnotherapy interesting. So I decided to investigate it more and came across Innervisions. As an intuitive I believe things cross your path at the right time. For me coming across Innervisions and hypnotherapy was the perfect time when I was ready to expand my knowledge. And I have loved every bit of it.

We build our reputation on your success

When I attended module one. I was quite nervous about stepping out of my comfort zone. But I needn't have been. The whole experience was absolutely mind blowing and left me wanting to learn more.
The people I met were all on their own journey but I felt we all had something special to offer. I felt comfortable and I found the whole experience brilliant. The way the information was given was easy to understand and just left me wanting to learn more. I left that weekend feeling excited for my new journey. And I couldn't wait to attend the next one.

The course itself I felt was interesting, informative and easy to understand. I felt it was actually a place of self discovery too. Because it allowed me to understand more about how my mind was working as well as the potential clients I would have in the future.

Every weekend brought something new and I was ready and eager to dive into learn more. My tutor made everything so interesting and I could see the passion within them for their work just made me want to be a part of that journey for myself.

I think I was already bitten by the bug so to speak. The amount of realisations you go through on the journey is mind blowing but in a positive way. And I was grateful to have such a wonderful tutor that had patience to help us all get through it in a fun and informative way. Just fabulous.

I love the post training support so much because I think this is where you can go into more depth. I love the supervision sessions and I have done many courses as extras too. The tutors are so knowledgeable and they are able to present each session in a way that I feel gives clear understanding of the subjects we cover. I think this is a vital part of becoming not just a good hypnotherapist, but becoming outstanding in your field.

We build our reputation on your success

My hypnotherapy practice enables me to pull all of my skills together. I work intuitively with my other therapies and have found that in some areas there is an overlap that seems to blend all of my skills together.

I love working with people to build their confidence and self esteem. Particularly with regard to anxiety and stress. Although I do cover many other areas too. And I aim to help people who see me feel at ease, this is a key area that is necessary to gain the trust between client and hypnotherapist.

I love my work and I love the transformations that can happen. My work is of service. And I am able to do this through my skills and talents as an intuitive, hypnotherapist and holistic therapist.

If I had one thing to offer to anyone who was thinking of changing direction in their lives I would say consider how much you could gain from learning and experiencing the amazing things hypnotherapy can offer. It's akin to transformation and who wouldn't want that if you could create a better life for yourself and others. Or at least guide someone else into finding it for themselves.

Love it all.

CHERYL LAWTON: MY POSITIVE HEALTH

I have spent my adult life working in healthcare as a Nurse, I'm in my 40th year. Over the years I have studied some complimentary therapies alongside the various courses I've attended in Nursing, and gaining complimentary therapies qualifications has often enhanced the care and support I have used for those in my care. For over the 40 years I have worked in a variety of specialities and healthcare settings, and most recently I have opened my own business which is a busy Ear Clinic. I see a fair proportion of my clients who have Tinnitus, which is unwanted noise that can be distressing, persistent and annoying, altering or affecting the hearing ability. One day I was particularly upset by the plight of a client, who confided in me that his Tinnitus had been so bad, that he felt like he was going mad, and was under the care of the Crisis team because he had contemplated suicide. I felt helpless and as Tinnitus is classed as permanent, I could see where he felt his options were limited, and I began to think how as an Ear clinic I could support Tinnitus Sufferers.

We build our reputation on your success

Some years ago I went for Hypnotherapy myself, and was treated successfully for a recurring nightmare I was having. I thought that Tinnitus too might be successfully treated as it is actually caused by the Brain. Amazingly, as this was on my mind, I saw the INNERVISIONS course advertised, and I decided to book my place. I wasn't at all wary about studying Hypnotherapy because I had been for hypnotherapy myself some years before. I had a really good outcome, which to this day has never occurred since.

Being in healthcare I was aware of various therapeutic interventions, and I was well aware of the power of the mind over the body to influence recovery and influence our health. I practiced meditation, and Reiki and was used to using my imagination in a therapeutic way, and therefore I kind of knew what to expect. I also had a friend who had done the very same course a few years before, and was pleasantly surprised how much more aware they were after it.

The INNERVISIONS course was very well put together, the topics were well organised into modules which progressed the learner deeper into the skills and techniques of hypnotherapy at just the right pace. There's an ideal balance of theory and practice it's very interactive. You can even be treated by your fellow students during the course, as you work together in the practical parts of the modules. I was released from the Bird phobia I had endured since being a child, and can now walk calmly through Pigeon flocks, and hold Owls without fear.

The way that the course is designed with attendance for one weekend every month allowed proper digestion of the course content, and resources, with time to practice the new skills and report back at the next monthly training to the Tutor and compare experiences with your peer group. The course tutors are appropriately experienced practitioners in their own right, and still actively delivering hypnotherapy in their own practices. They are able to demonstrate all the techniques and tools of hypnotherapy because they are using them and so it's all very natural and flowing. All the Tutors are trained in exactly the same way, and to all intents, with exactly the same content. INNERVISIONS uses it's own former students to teach the students of the future and in a way it's like passing down a family tradition. The process is proven over more than 25 years, and apart from minor improvements along the way, we have all received the same training.

From the moment you finish the course you are taken into the INNERVISIONS family. There are no cliques or ego's everybody has been through the same process and has most likely has had the same experiences along the way. There's a very active and supportive Facebook private group which is there 24/7 for any questions, ideas and information to be shared and responded to.

INNERVISIONS provides monthly supervision sessions which are delivered by a highly experienced team of tutors and practitioners who often have special expertise in particular areas of practice, but the sessions never seem formal or threatening the connection of the INNERVISIONS family always makes learning fun and worthwhile. CPD courses are also a means for the practitioners to learn advanced techniques that are a natural progression after the practitioner training, such as Parts Therapy, EFT, and Addictions.

I practice in Hull at my own clinic, and although I see clients for all aspects of hypnotherapy, I do specialise in supporting those with Tinnitus and have been successful in helping them to reduce and manage their condition better. I am pleased to say that one of those success stories was the original gentleman who set me on my hypnotherapy journey about 4 years ago.

MARY BLAKEY: MARY T BLAKEY THERAPY UK

I have always been intrigued by hypnotists and hypnotherapists and how hypnotherapy works and the power of the mind. I already incorporated visualisations, story telling and metaphors into my counselling practice. I saw an advert for a complimentary weekend with Innervisions and didn't think twice. After completing the complimentary weekend I was hooked and decided to train to be a hypnotherapist to compliment my business. I absolutely loved the training and became as passionate about hypnotherapy as I am about counselling. On attending module 1 I didn't know what to make of it or why anybody would offer a training weekend for free. I thought it might be a bit of a scam to be honest. However I soon realised it wasn't. The training was in a lovely hotel, with a very knowledgeable tutor, an abundance of information and with plenty of handouts. Our group was eager to learn and friendly and we were soon practising hypnotherapy on each other. Module 1 gave a lot of information about how hypnotherapy works in the brain and what hypnotherapy and being hypnotised is. The course was very informative and our tutor was amazing and as fascinating as the course content. She was very giving with her time and knowledge and made the learning fun. I honestly didn't want the course to end. Anything that she didn't already know, she took the time to find out for us. There is plenty of time to practice hypnotherapy on each other as a group which definitely helps. The course also gives help and guidance on setting up in practice and marketing. Post training there is an amazing closed Facebook group with Innervisions with an abundance of hypnotherapists from all over the country. You can post a question at any time of the day or night and within minutes a number of people will answer and will give guidance and advice on your query based on their own experience and practice. There is monthly supervision offered on line and plenty of training which is also now on line via zoom. The training is professionally delivered by Innervisions and often a book will compliment the training, sent via Amazon. You can also request a recording of the training to keep. I'm an Integrative and Client Centred Counsellor, Clinical Counselling Supervisor and a Clinical Hypnotherapist. I work creatively with adults and children. I have 16 years experience in the counselling field and in recent years added hypnotherapy to compliment my practice. Hypnotherapy uses hypnosis to work directly with the subconscious mind, facilitating you to make positive changes in your life. It can be a very quick and effective therapy which can help with a wide range of issues from phobias, trauma, anxiety, self improvement to weight loss or simply to help you to relax. I work creatively and I am very child focussed, although I also work with adults. I offer therapy at flexible times. Therapy sessions are available on line and in person. You are a unique individual and you deserve to live your best life.

JACQUELINE ANDERSON: ESSENCE HYPNOTHERAPY

Prior to being a hypnotherapist, I had been working in office management roles for over 25 years. I was approaching 50 and was feeling miserable and unfulfilled in my career so I made the decision to change direction. Office work had become mundane and boring but I had no idea what I wanted to do at that time, I felt like I was standing at a crossroads and had no idea which way to turn. Going back to college or university to retrain was out of the question as I needed to earn a full-time wage.

One evening, I just happened to be scrolling through Facebook when a post popped up about a free training weekend with Innervisions School of Clinical Hypnosis, so I requested further information. A short time after that I was contacted by one of the tutors for Innervisions and I signed up for the free weekend. After all, I had absolutely nothing to lose as the weekend was completely free.

We build our reputation on your success

I remember my Dad years ago talking about hypnosis as "a load of old baloney" and I have to say, I was sceptical for a while about this 'free weekend'. I had always been interested in the power of the mind and often used meditation for relaxation and studied neuroplasticity but I was a bit wary about hypnosis. Was there a hidden catch? Would there be a 'hard-selling' tactic involved to make me part with my hard-earned cash? Would I be 'hypnotised' out of money? Well fortunately, the answer to these questions is no. I was intrigued and wanted to find out more for myself, so I attended module one with a completely open mind. I have to say, I was pleasantly surprised. I took many 'gold nuggets' away with me from the free training and learned about the misconceptions surrounding hypnosis. It was a thoroughly enjoyable, fun weekend and I made the decision at the end of the second day that hypnotherapy was the way forward and I signed up for the full training course.

I started the course in 2018 but then had to defer my training for a few months due to my Dad passing away after a long illness. I re-joined for the second module in Leeds and then joined the Nottingham group with for the remainder of the course. Both tutors were brilliant, and along with my colleagues on the course they helped me through a particularly difficult time in my life. During the course my confidence improved considerably and I conquered my fear of motorway driving and flying. It was great being able to do the training at the weekend once a month, I was able to fit this in around my full-time job. I graduated with Innervisions in 2019.

There's lot's of support in the Innervisions group and also lots of opportunities for additional learning and training including new techniques and modalities. I did the EFT training, Parts training, Addictions training, Law of Attraction training and the Refresher training, to name a few. There is also the monthly supervision events that have covered a whole range of topics like training on using zoom and also marketing - which is essential for building a hypnotherapy business. There's lots of useful information on Hypnoflix.tv too, so there is support available for any issues or advice that you might need help with.

One of my favourite quotes is

"The energy of the mind is the essence of life" by Aristotle

and I decided to name my business Essence Hypnotherapy in 2019. My logo is a butterfly which symbolises transformation and resilience. In the latter part of the year I found premises in Ransom Wood, Mansfield, Nottingham. It is an idyllic place for therapies, my clinic is in a beautiful woodland setting surrounded by wildlife, it's a lovely environment to connect with nature.

The pandemic arrived shortly after I had set the business up and things were very tough for a while but we learned to pivot, adapt and evolve. As well as hypnotherapy I do EFT and alignment coaching, specialising in confidence and anxiety related issues. In the new year, my therapy dog Sirius will be joining me in the clinic, I'm really looking forward to that.

He will be providing support by helping clients with stress related issues. I left my full-time office job a few months ago to concentrate on my hypnotherapy business and now I absolutely love what I do. I have finally found my purpose in life.

PAUL TORRINGTON: EDWARD PAUL HYPNOTHERAPY

I worked as an apprentice mechanic and progressed through to Consultant Technical and then Manager. After many years I decided to change career paths and work for the NHS in a major hospital in the Clinical Engineering department, I currently still work part time there.

Part way through my motor trade years I suffered from a vertebrae problem in my lower back to which I was told was to risky to operate on and the only way forward was to take pain relief. This pain relief was in the form of high powered pain killers like tramadol, and after several years on these I became concerned of the damage they could be doing to me. So, I decided to look at alternative solutions. I did some research on hypnotherapy and it's ability to assist in this area, and had a few sessions with a chiropractor and then with a local hypnotherapist which worked fine and helped.

But mine was a long term issue, so when I saw by chance - (or was it fate?) the advertisement from 'Innervisions', for a trial weekend, I decided to take the bull by the horns and to train as a Clinical Hypnotherapist myself.

I have always genuinely loved working with people, and helping them, and being a clinical Hypnotherapist is all about helping people, and it's so rewarding when I see unfold in front of me the positive results and changes that it brings.

At first I was quite wary as unsure of what was involved or what I would actually be doing. Would I be suited to it? or indeed would I actually be capable of taking in the information and carrying out and applying what was learnt by putting the training into practice?

I needn't have worried, we were made to feel quite at ease, but also given essential ground rules that needed to be adhered to.

There were people from all walks of life, and a broad selection of age, but everyone was there for a reason, and were willing & wanted to learn.

The course was really constructive, open to discussion in depth, with lots of practical hands on work. even at that early stage I could see and feel that we were starting to gel into a 'Hypno family' - everyone supported each other, shared life experiences, & I feel developed into better people.

The training is quite intense at times and can be mentally exhausting too, but it was always enjoyable. Our Tutor really was excellent! he lived and breathed the training, and put 100% into everything. He made it fun, but was also quite serious in the places he needed to be.

He put the training into bite size chunks, and offered up examples, if we were struggling with anything in particular he would take time to ensure this was rectified.

We build our reputation on your success

The post training support is excellent! Complimented with regular supervision and study sessions on a wide variety of subjects. These regularly include a guest a speaker.

But, there is also actually so much resource and support that is available and readily given by everyone on the Innervisions therapy community site. This site has become invaluable, we can run ideas by each other, share experiences, gain ideas and more knowledge, it really is a big Innervisions hypnotherapy family.

I currently run my sessions from a room at home as I have ample parking, privacy & access, in comfortable and relaxing surroundings. In summer it's even possible to conduct them outside in a quiet garden area overlooking fields & countryside. but also occasionally I go mobile to a clients own home as a number of people seem to prefer this initially.

I've have great success with various issues. For example sleep problems, stress, anxiety, to sports enhancements and concentration, pain management exam revision, fear of flying/driving etc etc to name a few. advise.

HELEN JANE: HELEN JANE HYPNOTHERAPY

Whilst working for British Airways as long-haul cabin crew I sustained a serious back injury which resulted in surgery. I was referred to a pain management specialist to help with the chronic pain. After a few sessions I was pain free. I didn't know it at the time however this was my first experience of hypnosis. As a result of the injury, I was forced to change career and decided to retrain as a life coach and mental health practitioner. I loved working with people with mental health issues using my life coaching and Cognitive Behavioural Therapy skills whilst they waited for counselling. Over time I noticed that many people came back into service with the same issues time after time or that counselling, CBT, and life coaching just did not help. It became apparent that, for some, additional support was needed. I started to research and became fascinated with the power of the unconscious mind. This led to me deciding to train as a hypnotherapist so that I could work with my clients on a deeper level to make lasting change.

I was excited to attend module one. I was open minded and intrigued. Having already researched hypnotherapy and having experienced the benefit of hypnosis in pain management I was curious if I would be able to incorporate hypnotherapy into my practice to support my clients. My main concern was how I would fit the training in around working full time. After learning how the modules were delivered, I decided this would not be an obstacle to my training to become a hypnotherapist.

I really enjoyed attending module one. It was helpful to meet the tutor and to gain insight into the training. Any concerns that students had were fully addressed and I felt so confident in the Innervisions' training that I signed up without hesitation.

The course is very well structured. It takes you on a pathway from no knowledge to having the confidence, skills, and knowledge to set up a hypnotherapy practice.

Having the monthly sessions enabled me to work through the content at my own pace and then bring any questions to the sessions. There was no such thing as a stupid question.

Throughout the training I felt fully supported and encouraged by the tutor. The tutor was very knowledgeable and supportive and brought valuable experience of running her own successful practice to the sessions.

The content was delivered professionally and at an appropriate pace.

There were plenty of opportunities to ask questions and ample time for practice sessions to help build confidence. I particularly enjoyed the workshops which meant that I had the tools and the confidence to begin running sessions as soon as I had qualified.

The post training support has been excellent. It really does feel as though you are part of a family. It is so helpful to be able to tap into the experience and support of other more experienced hypnotherapists.

We build our reputation on your success

There is ample opportunity to attend additional trainings to further your knowledge and refresher training to brush up on your skills should you need it.
Opportunities for monthly supervision with expert speakers are offered which are also very helpful.

I feel totally supported in the knowledge that I can ask for advice and support when needed.

I love working with midlife women.

Midlife can be a challenging time for many women with lots of changes, both expected and unexpected. Women often feel stuck, lost, unseen and unheard, unsure of the way forward as they deal with lack of purpose, burnout, health issues, relationship breakdown, empty nesting, bereavement, career change and redundancy.

Over the years I have worked with 100's of women using a variety of therapies including hypnotherapy, life coaching, EFT and energy alignment to support them in moving forward.

I offer a bespoke service tailored to the needs of the individual. This often includes work around menopause, weight management, health issues, pain management, anxiety, stress, confidence, and sleep. I also offer group sessions and online courses.

DONNA GALLOWAY: SEVEN HILLS WELLBEING CENTRE

Previously I worked as a sales merchandiser for a blue-chip company for many years. Life was becoming very repetitive and uninteresting. Therefore, I needed to do something about it. I decided to change career for a more fulfilled lifestyle. I saw the Innervisions School of Clinical Hypnosis advertisement on Facebook and something clicked. I was intrigued. As the first workshop was free I thought that I would give it a go. It wasn't going to cost me anything for the weekend except time.

However, I didn't expect to be so pleasantly surprised and pleased with the weekend course and waited with anticipation to hear if I had been accepted into the full course.

On the first morning of the free weekend, I felt so nervous and I must admit even a little sceptical. I had always enjoyed the hypnotist on TV and was about to find out more about the secrets of the hypnotic world.

We build our reputation on your success

Little did I know that I was about to change my life forever. The other students on the course were from all different walks of life. Different abilities and reasons for being there. However that didn't matter at all, they were a very friendly group of people. The free foundation weekend was well put together, informative, enjoyable and the weekend went very fast. We learned of the history of hypnotherapy and the misleading information regarding the subject. We even got to practice on each other.

I can't praise the course enough really, it was a 10 month course packed with lots of reading, discussions, practical exercises and sessions.

During the course we developed the skills needed to competent and confident hypnotherapists. You could ask the tutor any questions and they be answered fully from a knowledgeable tutor. The only silly question is the one you don't ask.' This is so true. It really didn't matter how many we asked, so long as we understood. Some of the people I met on the course have become very good friends and the ones who lived further afield, there's always Facebook. After you graduate and set up your business, it can be quite daunting. However once qualified you will be invited into a private group for professional hypnotherapists. This group is invaluable. The camaraderie, kindness and helpfulness of those who are in the group never ceases to amaze me. There is always someone online to help you though your questions and advise you on the best way to help your clients and business. Even if you don't have a question to ask, following the conversation on different approaches and subjects reinforces the training you received during the course. I'd definitely recommend that you join the group once invited.

I had a wish to open my own Wellbeing Centre. A place for all different holistic therapies with Hypnotherapy being the main practice. Fortunately I have now achieved that. It was a 3 year journey from first seeing the perfect building for my venture, as someone else ran a business from there, to now being proud of what I have achieved.

VIVIENNE RAWNSLEY:

Working in education, as a teacher in both special needs and mainstream schools, for over 30 years I had developed an interest in the workings of the human mind and how events from the past can get locked in our subconscious mind affecting the choices we make in the present and the future. Having personally experienced the impact of hypnosis following a traumatic divorce I expanded my learning further and decided to train as a clinical hypnotherapist.

Training as a hypnotherapist gave me a key to unlocking the power of our subconscious minds and transform life as we know it.

I attended the first weekend training sessions with an open mind as an opportunity to further my personal and professional development. During module one the experience I had being hypnotised together with training I had engaged in as a neuro linguistic programming practitioner fell into place. I was excited by what I was learning and

drawn further into the world of clinical hypnotherapy. The tutor and training material were informative and engaging.
This supported my decision of, rather than enrolling in an online course offering no post qualification support or business development training, to enrol with the INNERVISIONS school of clinical hypnosis.

I found the INNERVISIONS training to be extremely high quality. The combination of theory and practical sessions, during which each student experienced and used each technique and process, was a great combination and supported each of the trainees in gaining confidence as they became clinical hypnotherapists. Working together developed the skills of each individual as the high quality tutor monitored the practical application of the theory that he had shared with us. The course material was easy to access for all learning styles with additional support for those trainees who felt less confident in their abilities. Each student experienced elements of the hypnosis training and this impacted their confidence and other areas of their personal development.

Post training support has included opportunities to engage in supervision as required by the General Hypnotherapy Council.

Additional training has also been available as support for gaining additional skills in specific areas. These have included both hypnosis techniques and business development. Training that I have engaged in has included Law of Attraction, Emotional Freedom Technique, Addictions, Parts Therapy, How to use Facebook and Facebook adds, Using audible to create professional hypnosis recordings using audible and Hypnoslimmer. I work with clients both face to face and online to support them in experiencing change in their lives. Much of the work I do involves overcoming trauma. This ranges from small seemingly insignificant incidents that have impacted the clients subconscious mind to affect how they regard themselves and their world, to life changing events that shake the clients world result in them struggling to exist beyond it. Hypnotherapy is blended with other tools to create

We build our reputation on your success

bespoke packages that support the clients in making changes in their lives, resulting in increased confidence, happiness, personal and professional opportunities, satisfaction and success.

MICHELE KNOTT SIMEY:

After absolutely hating school for the whole of my childhood, I somehow found myself as a teaching assistant. With 11 years under my belt a change in management found me questioning my commitment to teaching. I was always the "go to" person for comfort and advice so I started to consider retraining as a counsellor or therapist. I wasn't really sure which course to take or where to look for guidance so I decided to rely on my instincts and wait for a "sign" to help me decide. It wasn't too long before I noticed a post on social media regarding Innervisions hypnotherapy training. I read and reread the advert and something just clicked. I enquired the very next day. After a chat with the course tutor over the phone, I was invited to attend a free training weekend at a local hotel. When I arrived at the venue I met several other people and we got chatting. We all wondered what we might expect but I just had a good feeling about it. The tutor called us through, introduced herself and explained the shape of the weekend before allowing us all to get acquainted over refreshments. On that very first morning I knew I'd found my path, I belonged. The whole weekend flew by in what seemed like seconds, I was hooked. The best part of course was it was completely free!

My tutor was Lynn Appleyard, a brilliantly engaging teacher who puts across content in such a way that you barely notice that you're being educated. The modules are absolutely fascinating and I can honestly say I've never enjoyed a course as much as this one.

We all qualified together in a lovely party atmosphere in the hotel, followed by a celebratory dinner in a local hostelry! Post qualification, we were all transferred from our original media support group to the amazing Innervisions group. I for one have used the group for advice and I hope I've also given support. It's also a great place tell each other about our wins! All of the supervision opportunities are posted within the group and delivered via Zoom. This makes things accessible for all. What's also great is that all of the course tutors hang out in the group ready to impart their extensive knowledge whenever we may falter.
As soon as I was confident in my ability I left my day job and set up my therapy room at home. I wanted the space to feel calm and comfortable and with a sumptuous chair, soft throws, beautiful artwork and peaceful music I achieved my dream. I now work with people who suffer from anxiety, low self esteem, insomnia, lack of confidence, who would like to stop smoking or would like to weigh less. I just love being a hypnotherapist and have never once looked back.

I'm so glad that Brian Glenn decided he wanted to help a million people and although he may have meant hypnotherapy clients, indirectly I am one of his million! Thanks Brian x

SUE FERGUSON: SUE FERGUSON HYPNOTHERAPY

I am a nurse who still works part time so deal with people from a physical model. I always felt like there was more to life than just physical health and quite by accident I came upon the free weekend with Innervisions . I was intrigued by the content of the course and also by the others who attended that free weekend. Something was ignited within me , I could sense this was the answer to what I was looking for so decided to sign up for the course.

My fellow students , along with the fabulous tutors soon turned my life upside down. I found out more about myself in those months of training than I knew existed!!! The training changed me as a person (for the better) and gave me amazing skills that I now use not only with my hypnotherapy clients but I also apply the knowledge that the mind is capable of so much more than we possibly give it credit for in dealing with patients.
To use the skills to help an individual to change their life and to see life from a different perspective is truly a gift . All thanks to Innervisions.

We build our reputation on your success

I was the tutors worse nightmare as I was so sceptical. I asked so many questions and challenged just about everything. I was probably the most annoying student in the room. As a nurse the things that were presented to me sort of challenged my perception of life and the 'way things were'. I found the other students intriguing, so many different people with such different view points and beliefs. I was sure I wouldn't have anything in common with them. How wrong I was about everything. They became good friends , we all shared a lot, both in the lecture rooms and out !!!! I grew as a person and quite honestly can say the course changed me for the better and I haven't looked back since.

I wouldn't be the person I am today without the Innervisions course and I even got the certificate for the most improved student 😌

My tutors were so enthusiastic about the course content. They delivered it in an easy to understand and enlightening way. Their knowledge and enthusiasm was infectious, making each weekend informative and fun. We did have so much fun!!! I can honestly say I looked forward to each weekend with delight.

The content of the course was presented in a professional manner and full information was given as to what to expect, what was expected of you and how to achieve the best in yourself.

Being able to put into practice what you had learned each weekend was invaluable . The practical work and theory were complimentary.

Once qualifying it's a scary thing to start seeing clients initially but the best aspect of Innervisions is the support provide on line with the Innervisions support group . You are able to post queries about anything without the fear of being judged . You gain insight into others practice just by reading the different posts from newly qualified and those who have been around a bit longer. No question is too big or too small and you are never made to feel like your question is irrelevant. Lots of information about courses, supervision, and articles are provided to access continuously. You feel as if you are not alone as you go along your own journey.

I only see a few clients at the moment as I still work as a nurse part time.

I have a small converted room at home which I currently use as a therapy room . I am having an extension built to provide more space . I see a whole range of client issues from slimming to anxiety, from stopping smoking to IBS.

Clients are generally from word of mouth (I do find the marketing aspect slightly daunting) I have developed my own programme for IBS symptom relief and am keen to specialise in this area of hypnotherapy. I would like to eventually give up nursing to devote more time to my hypnotherapy clients.

CAROLLE WESTBURY: INSIDE MIND HYPNOTHERAPY

I loved the idea of helping a variety of people through the wonderful world of hypnotherapy. I have always been the person where people have gravitated to for emotional and practical help, and eventually realised that this was what one of my highest values was. It gives me great pleasure to be involved, and to meet such a variety of people. Who are each fascinating in their own individual ways. The sense of satisfaction when a person has been set free from an issue or problem that has previously been hampering their happiness and well being is second to none. My career has previously been is sales management which is in essence fulfilling a customers needs, and I believe hypnotherapy has a similar purpose.

I attended module one feeling very nervous, but curious about learning about the world of hypnotherapy. It was an enlightening and enjoyable experience, which gave a fascinating insight into the human brain. I did think that I would probably only attend for one day of the two day course, but I can honestly say I was hooked after the initial introduction and could not wait to attend day two. On the second day we were taken deeper into the training and given wonderful insights into hypnotherapy and its power. The end of that day was completed with a practical demonstration which was truly awe inspiring.

On my course we unfortunately lost our initial trainer, but the transition to our new trainer Laura was absolutely seamless, and I felt completely supported throughout the whole process. We were informed at the very beginning of the course that our lives would change as a result of the course, and how true that information was!

There is plenty of support after qualification. With an online community, and direct messaging to anyone within the group. There are regular supervision courses via zoom, and there is also forums for discussion and assistance. There are also other courses on offer which enable one to delve deeper into subjects such as parts therapy, addictions, and pain management. At the end of the course and on the last weekend of graduation we were advised how to set up a hypnotherapy practice, and guided towards the correct bodies with which to be involved in. There is always someone to turn to for advice and help. The family of Innervisions hypnotherapy is certainly very embracing and supportive.

My practice is conducted both face to face and via zoom. I'm happy to work in whatever way is best for my clients. Although I am perfectly happy to treat a variety of problems and issues, the majority of my work so far has been in the area of fears and phobias. I am very grateful and humbled to have quite a lot of recommendations in this sphere, and my clients are certainly ecstatic to shed unwanted thoughts and feelings.

LEAH GOODALL: LEAH GOODALL HYPNOTHERAPY

I have spent the first 25 years of my career in finance, specifically debt chasing and I enjoy driving fast cars in my spare time and part time. During those years I met my wonderful husband who is an ex royal marine commando. Over the years the signs of PTS(d) began to show in him but soldiers don't often talk and almost always refuse therapy, it's ingrained in them to 'crack on'. I sought out a therapy that could help him where almost nothing needs to be said, just a few small positive solution focused questions. I found hypnotherapy. I found Innervisions School of clinical hypnosis. The free weekend changed my life. I attended the free weekend in Nottingham in 2019 with an open mind and a hope that I had found a solution. The energy in the room over the weekend is amazing. The structure of the course is well laid out and very easy to understand and follow and the more you learn the more exciting the day becomes. The tutors are amazing, funny and so full of knowledge, able to answer even the most bizarre questions. It didn't feel like school, it was fun and entertaining right through to the end and i walked away knowing how to perform hypnosis. I was very blessed to be able to return to the school a few years later and aid one of the diplomas alongside my former tutor. I trained at the lace market. The rooms were very large and clean with excellent facilities, tea, coffee, juice, biscuits and cakes all laid on. Our tutor brought the science behind the myths, the facts and evidence and headed the classes. The students I trained with are from all around the world which brought amazing insight into cultural beliefs and different kinds of clients that may walk through our doors. We practiced on each other and as a result have all become life long friends who meet regularly for social CPD. The thing that I love most about my training with Innervisions is that it never ended, I joined a family. The online support that we all give each other is second to none. We all join other groups but the skill level of the therapists through the years, the monthly supervision, the more in depth subjects, watching each other bloom and choose paths to specialise in, the sharing of clients, therapy swapping with each other, the list of support is endless.

I have been seeing hypnotherapy clients for 9 years now. I don't advertise. I enjoy being out on the open roads so I have a part time day job driving fast cars and I see all of my clients by referral only. I started small with friends and family as trust was already there, who went on and told their friends and family and now I see 4 clients a week, because I choose to. Financially I've never been able to say that before. I set aside 8 hours over two days. I have converted a bedroom in my home into my studio and I visited local therapists with clinics and sourced places that felt right for me and my clients. I specialise with depression, anxiety, PTS(d) and stress related clients but really enjoy the journeys I take with my HypnoSlimmer clients, their results are always so amazing. I'm not conventional, I don't ask for reviews and with weight change its so easy to see it happen it lifts my soul.

KELLY KING: BE FREE CLINICAL HYPNOTHERAPY

I was diagnosed with a genetic condition and suffered crippling chronic health from the age of 40, & early onset menopause. I enrolled with Innversions in 2019 to make changes to my health and life. As I learnt, I healed, then I wanted to help others through my new knowledge and life experience. Sadly Covid held me back and knocked my confidence and self esteem. It's coming to the end of 2021, Covid is still prevalent, but it's no longer holding me back. I am now in a position to offer my hypnotherapy services as an on-line therapist or in person.

I went along to the free foundation weekend in Sheffield during September, thinking I wasn't good enough or even clever enough and full of self doubt and limiting beliefs. But I should have left all of that doubt at the front door. I had the most amazing weekend. I was absolutely buzzing. I had seen the most amazing things happen, there, right in front of my eyes. I loved everything about the weekend, the like minded people who were there with me. The quality of

We build our reputation on your success

information, the delivery of the information, the demonstrations, everything. Quite simply, I was hooked, line and sinker.

I absolutely loved the professional relationship I had with my tutor. He and his assistant, presented and assisted the course with maximum effect. Nothing was too much trouble to re-explain or offer a more in-depth explanation at any stage. Our homework, course work and practice sessions, were always of a high professional standard, with enough time or more if needed, to practice to the fullest extent. He was professional at all times, friendly, approachable and full of hypnotherapy life experience and knowledge. There was always an opportunity to ask him anything and he would always guide and support us where necessary.

The post training experiences have been to the highest standard with Brian and or members of his team. I have undertaken a hypnotherapy refresher course to boost my confidence and self esteem (due to graduating during Covid) and further training with the Emotional Freedom Technique course and the Law of Attraction course which were both amazing and have given me the opportunity to use with clients. This is a very exciting time for me. I now see Covid as a pause in my life and practice, whereby I had the opportunity to gain extra experience and more knowledge from Innervisions. I am launching my new hypnotherapy practice (post covid) to help my wider community and also specialising in midlife issues, The Menopause and past Traumas.

A very warm thank you to Brian for being a part of his amazing warm Innervisions family. I know that I can come to Brian and his Team and/or the Facebook Group with any query or question and I know it will be answered quickly with a resolution.

LEANNE DEWEY: MADE MINDSET

The power of the mind has always intrigued me, I truly believe with the right mindset that anything is possible!

Hypo-Coaching is tied with practical strategies and powerful and effective techniques, adding another dimension to traditional hypnotherapy and coaching. Working with both the conscious and subconscious mind allows you to make deeper, longer lasting changes, from the inside out. My passion has always been to help people, who are ready to help themselves and this absolutely can do that! I attended module one with an open mind and saw it as an learning weekend, I'm a sucker for courses so was not something new to me. The weekend was very informative and I learnt so much over the two days, when I got home I started consuming as much information as I could about the power of hypnosis and it didn't take me long to know this was the path for me!
I loved that the course was offered as a free weekend to begin and there was no pressure to join which to me is a good quality.

The course in general is very good, there is plenty to learn and an array of areas covered. There is definitely enough material to set up your practice and get going straight after the course including the relevant business information needed. I liked the variety of practical and theory learning, the balance was just right to allow you to gain the knowledge needed but also build confidence in your own ability as an hypnotherapist. Our tutor was very helpful and supportive to everyone on the course - I do like to ask a lot of questions and he was able to answer everyone I had :)

After the training we was invited to join the community group which has many files, scripts that can aid you in your own business. There is also the support to ask questions and get other peoples points of view and there recommendations which is a real nice to have if you are presented with a pain point that you haven't had much experience with in the past. I'm an Internationally Accredited Transformation Coach, Accredited Clinical Hypnotherapist, Mum and Life Junkie!

I specialise in helping self-doubting women who know they want more, find their confidence and self worth, remove limiting beliefs that are holding them back and develop a powerful mindset that works for them!

I'm obsessed with helping ladies all over the world reach their full potential whilst enjoying the journey to get there. I help my clients achieve their personal goals on a 1:1 basis, with my full support and accountability I promise you, that you can too achieve whatever in life you want, on your own terms!

POTENTIAL EARNINGS

WHAT CAN A HYPNOTHERAPIST EARN?

Hypnotherapy is a fulfilling, challenging, and rewarding occupation, but can you earn enough to support you? It's an important question, because unless you can make a good living as a hypnotherapist, you won't be able to replace your current income or make enough money to live on. Also, is it worth the initial cost of the training too?

When you look up "how much does a hypnotherapist earn" you'll see the figure of £48,037, but as you are unlikely to find a role as an employed hypnotherapist, it might be more helpful to look at "how much does a self-employed hypnotherapist earn" because you'll almost certainly be running your own private practice.

The average cost of a hypnotherapy session in the UK is £75 per hour with most charging between £50 and £90 per session. You'll be setting your own fees and there are factors which will influence the price, which I'll go into more detail later.

Before that, let's project two different scenarios which are common to many people working as hypnotherapists.

WORKING PART-TIME

The first is someone who wants to fit their practice around their life, children or other responsibilities.

They charge £75 per session, see 10 paying clients per week and take 12 weeks off per year. This would mean they would turn over £750 per week, equating to £30,000 per year before tax and expenses.

The great thing about hypnotherapy is that you can fit this business around you and it is a business that can change according to your needs.

WORKING FULL-TIME

Scenario two, in which someone wants to devote a significant proportion of each week to their business. This time they see 20 clients per week and take 6 weeks off per year. They would turn over £1500 per week, equating to £69,000 per year.

In addition to client-facing time, you'll need to allocate a percentage of your time to marketing, administration and finances. A good average is approximately 20% of client time for each task. The part-time hypnotherapist would allocate a further 6 hours, whereas the full-time hypnotherapist would allocate a further 12 hours.

Many people work far longer in their current jobs, which might be why people enjoy being a hypnotherapist so much! When you can make a significant impact on the well-being of people, make a good living and have the time and energy to enjoy your life then you'll enjoy your career too.

HOW MUCH DOES IT COST TO RUN A HYPNOTHERAPY BUSINESS?

There are costs involved in running any business and running a hypnotherapy business is no different. This may affect how much you charge or how many client hours you choose to offer. As it can vary depending on your life, where you live and other commitments or income, this can only be a guide. It's useful to think about the following:

WORKING FROM HOME VS RENTED OFFICE

Insurance – ~£80 per year
Professional Association membership – ~£100 each
Supervision – this is a requirement of professional practice and costs upwards of £20-£40 per month (£10 with Innervisions).

Continued Professional Development (CPD) – you're expected to keep up to date by doing several CPD hours each year. This could include watching a documentary, reading a book, meeting up with peers and attending formal training.

Subscriptions for magazines, booking software, design software etc – varies and depends on what, if any, services you use.

Networking costs – this can vary from a casual free meetup where you just pay for coffee, to membership and meeting fees for formal networking.

Other marketing costs – website, leaflets and business cards, advertising on/offline.

Book keeping/accountancy costs – these vary greatly and you could of course choose to do your own if able.

This might seem like a long list, but running a hypnotherapy business is, in practice, fairly simple. Like anything, there seems a lot to learn at the start, but once you know what you're doing, it becomes easier.

HOW MUCH SHOULD YOU CHARGE FOR HYPNOTHERAPY?

How much you charge for hypnotherapy sessions, depends on several factors, such as how much you need to earn, how many sessions you want to offer each week, how much your costs are, your experience and what package your client is having. To a lesser extent, it might include your location in the UK and your competitors' prices but those should not be deciding factors.

The first thing to decide is how much you would like to earn as a hypnotherapist. Start with the end in mind. You may have an aspirational goal or want to replace an employed income.

Bear in mind you'll need to work out the costs of doing business – a rough guide is 50% of the money you make is your 'salary' – the rest is for expenses for the business, tax and some business savings. Whilst this is not an exact metric, it at least helps you start thinking about how much you want to turnover.

Estimate the costs associated with doing business and the number of hours you have available each week to devote to running your business. When you decide how much you want to make, how much it costs and how many hours you want to work each week and how many weeks each year, you can work out an hourly rate.

This can be a helpful exercise, as many therapists undercharge, not realising their fees don't cover everything needed to run a business and survive.

At the start of your hypnotherapy career, you may do some launch discounts, contra deals (to offer services to the value of reciprocal services), special offers and maybe free work, to get your name out there and testimonials.

Your training will have set you up to be a competent hypnotherapist, so you should not discount due to the quality of your therapy, but sometimes you may choose to work at a slightly lower fee whilst you build your confidence. There is no requirement or encouragement to do this; you have many hours of real-world experience even before you qualify and you are worth what you charge.

It used to be that if you lived in the south you would charge significantly more than the same hypnotherapist living in the north; this is less true than it has ever been but may still factor to a lesser degree, particularly if you live in a city where costs are higher or want to work with a particular section of the community where their income is generally lower.

Many hypnotherapists now work online and therefore have a worldwide potential client base so where you live is becoming less and less of a consideration in setting your fees.

It can be an idea if you do want to do low-cost or charitable work, to have two sets of fees – one for most people and one for your low-cost work. Some hypnotherapists like to offer discounts to blue light services or armed forces personnel – it's totally up to you. It's your business and you can choose to help whoever you want, just remember you have a cost of living too.

Some treatments, such as smoking, are a single, longer session and you may choose to charge a slightly higher price for this, as there is no ongoing engagement but its results are life changing.

Some people think you should charge less for online versus face-to-face sessions; we believe this is not true because there are costs involved in running a business from anywhere and the service is no less valuable because there is no in-person clinic. You, however, may think differently.

The wonderful thing about running your own business is that you set the rules; if you want to give discounts to teachers in your local area because you were a teacher and know the pressure or create a package for police officers attempting to pass a bleep test you can.

Doing work that gives your life meaning and positively impacts your community, while you make a good living, is what we all aspire to.

EQUAL OPPORTUNITIES

All applicants will receive consideration for a place on our Practitioner Level Training Course without regard to race, colour, religion, gender, gender identity or expression, sexual orientation, national origin, genetics, disability, age, or veteran status.

Whilst academic qualifications may be an advantage, we regard it as only being a small part of the learning curve to becoming a competent clinical hypnotherapist. This hypnotherapy training course is therefore open to those with a genuine interest in hypnotherapy even though they may not have any relevant prior learning or training.

As a caring training provider, it is not uncommon for us to allow certain people to attend our course at a reduced fee, or even free of charge if we feel they have the life skills and passion that is conducive to our profession, but do not have the financial resources to pay. Please note however that this is strictly at the discretion of the tutor and Principal and free and subsidised places will only be awarded if we feel the student meets our strict criteria.

Please also note that the student will be protected by our strict codes of confidentiality.

WHAT NEXT?

Every single day, Hypnotherapists worldwide are making a massive impact on the lives of fellow human beings by helping them resolve the wounds and struggles of modern day living.

Furthermore; by becoming a Clinical Hypnotherapist, you get to play in the fascinating space of human potential. You get to explore the power of the human mind and witness what it can do to overcome physical, mental and emotional concerns. And as part of this process, you will evolve as a human being yourself.

If you have not yet enrolled on our practitioner level course, go to our website and take advantage of our Module One discount.

www.innervisions.co.uk

We build our reputation on your success

TRAIN FOR A REWARDING NEW CAREER AS A CLINICAL HYPNOTHERAPIST

We are currently looking for compassionate caring individuals who love helping people. We are offering a discounted Foundation Hypnotherapy Training Weekend via our unique tried and tested Interactive Virtual Classroom powered by Zoom, so that you can experience the power of clinical hypnosis and also find out for yourself if hypnotherapy is the right career choice for you.

Every single day, Hypnotherapists worldwide are making a massive impact by helping people resolve the wounds of modern day living, and traumatic issues from their past. And with all the physical and psychological challenges facing everyone right now, there's never been a better time to train.

If you're curious about doing the same, join us on our next intake, and very soon you could be helping people in need and enjoying a satisfying, lucrative and rewarding new career as a professional Clinical Hypnotherapist.

With over 29 years of experience, we consider ourselves to be Europe's leading Hypnotherapy Training Provider.

We aim to be the best in our particular field and to surpass our student's expectations; our teaching methods are unique, supportive, warm and friendly. We are dedicated to this profession, and we intend to assist and train each student to become a competent practitioner in modern clinical hypnosis and hypnotherapy.

The course is designed to be of particular relevance to those in the caring profession as well as anyone who has an interest in the field of human potential and personal development. Whilst academic qualifications may be an advantage, we regard it as only being a small part of the learning curve to becoming a competent clinical hypnotherapist. This hypnotherapy training course is therefore open to those with a genuine interest in hypnotherapy irrespective of race, religion, and environmental classification, even though they may not have any relevant prior learning or training.

ACCREDITATION

Our practitioner level training course has been assessed and validated at practitioner level by The General Hypnotherapy Standards Council (UK). Graduates are eligible for professional registration with The General Hypnotherapy Register at full practitioner status.

www.innervisions.co.uk

Printed in Great Britain
by Amazon